LEGO® NINJAGO™
Masters of Spinjitzu

NINJA VS. GHOST NINJA

WRITTEN BY
CLAIRE SIPI

A NEW GHOSTLY THREAT

IN SEASON FIVE of NINJAGO™ : Masters of Spinjitzu, a threat rises like none before. Ghosts swarm over Ninjago Island, possessing one ninja and turning another into a ghost! Old foes return, and the ninja need all the help they can get to counter Morro, the Master of Wind. A total of 18 LEGO® sets bring you thrilling minifigures and weapons that are bigger than any before!

HOW TO USE THIS BOOK

This book is a guide to the LEGO® NINJAGO™ minifigures of Season 5. Learn all about the ninja's ghoulish enemies and the new abilities they must achieve in order to defeat them.

To find out more about this minifigure see p.21.

CONTENTS

DEEPSTONE NINJA

WAGING GHOST WARS

New double-layered, two-colored zukin headwrap

Green Ninja's elemental symbol on front of torso, with his Creation emblem on the back

Straps and belt in ninja's personal color

DEEPSTONE STYLE

Lloyd's Deepstone minifigure appears in two sets. He comes with his new zukin headwrap and his distinctive blond hairpiece for two interchangeable looks.

HAVING DEFEATED THE ANACONDRAI, Lloyd and his fellow ninja must now face the treacherous Morro and his Ghost Army. Lloyd is fired up to save Ninjago Island from these ghoulish creatures, but is his new Deepstone armor enough to protect him from the dark forces at work?

EVIL GREEN NINJA

POSSESSED!

Jagged-edged zukin headwrap with green bandana face mask attached

Sword of Sanctuary

FRIEND OR FOE?

The Evil Green Ninja attacks the ninja on the *Destiny's Bounty*, and tries to steal the Staff of the First Master of Spinjitzu. In a battle with Kai, the Master of Fire is able to momentarily remind Lloyd of his true self, before Morro takes control again.

DID YOU KNOW?

The Sword of Sanctuary has the power of precognition, which means the possessor of it can see into the future.

LLOYD BECOMES the evil Green Ninja when Morro possesses him. Manipulative Morro tricks Lloyd into a meeting at the Ninjago Museum of History and then takes control of his body. Lloyd takes on the ghoulish features of his possessor, and wears sinister, tattered robes.

DEEPSTONE JAY

GHOST HUNTER

DEEPSTONE JAY

NINJA FILE

LIKES: Eerie tombs
DISLIKES: Deadly tests
FRIENDS: Scaredy cat Cole
FOES: Bansha
SKILLS: Protecting friends
GEAR: Deepstone Nunchuk

SET NAME: Jay Walker One, City of Stiix, Attack of the Morro Dragon, Titan Mech Battle, Temple of Airjitzu
SET NUMBER: 70731, 70732, 70736, 70737, 70751
YEAR: 2015

DID YOU KNOW?

Deepstone, mined from the bottom of the ocean, is an effective material used in both combat and defense against the ghosts.

Two shurikens slot into belt

Deepstone Nunchuck

HAUNTED GATEWAY

Jay must get to the Haunted Gateway and grab the Aeroblade before Morro's ghost troops overpower him and turn him into a ghost, too!

WIELDING HIS DEEPSTONE Nunchuks at lightning speed, Jay is a formidable force. Kitted out in his sleek, protective robe and armor, Jay is calm and focused on his mission to get the Scroll of Airjitzu and to take on the testing challenges of the Haunted Temple.

DEEPSTONE KAI

AQUAPHOBIC

NINJA FILE

LIKES: Saving Lloyd
DISLIKES: Water
FRIENDS: Possessed Lloyd
FOES: Morro
SKILLS: Trusting his friends
GEAR: Deepstone Scythe

SET NAME: City of Stiix, Attack of the Morro Dragon, Temple of Airjitzu
SET NUMBER: 70732, 70736, 70751
YEAR: 2015

Zukin headwrap in Kai's signature red color

Deepstone Scythe

Kai's elemental symbol is on the front of torso and his fire emblem on the back.

DID YOU KNOW?

The Aeroblades, circular shuriken-like weapons, have the ability to defeat the ghosts when they come into contact with them.

TOMB RAIDERS

Kai jumps on his speedy jet board to try and intercept the terrifying Morro Dragon. Kai hopes to stop the Evil Green Ninja from stealing the Realm Crystal from the tomb of the First Spinjitzu Master.

FIERY KAI will do anything (even if it means overcoming his fear of water!) to save his friend Lloyd. Armed with his Deepstone Scythe, Kai marches to Stiix to take on the might of the Ghost Army and destroy Morro and his ghostly thugs.

DEEPSTONE ZANE

NINDROID VS. GHOSTS

NINJA FILE

LIKES: Fighting ghosts
DISLIKES: Wrayth's noisy
ghost cycle
FRIENDS: Hot-headed Kai
FOES: Wrayth
SKILLS: Controlling the
Titan Mech
GEAR: Aeroblade

SET NAME: Titan Mech
Battle, Temple of Airjitzu
SET NUMBER: 70737,
70751
YEAR: 2015

Aeroblade—
when touched
it glows!

New black ninja robe with
body armor made from
Deepstone material protects
the wearer from being
possessed by the ghosts.

TITAN MECH BATTLE

Sitting in the cockpit of his Titan Mech,
Zane is set for the ultimate Mech
battle. He uses the awesome weapons
of his mighty machine to fight the
terrifying four-armed Ghost Mech,
Mech-enstein!

THE TITANIUM NINJA is back in style!
As cool as his icy element in his new
Deepstone gear, Zane uses his superior
robotic intelligence, stamina, and sixth
sense to the max to tackle and outwit the
ghostly enemy. With an Aeroblade at his
command, Zane is armed and dangerous!

GHOST VS. GHOSTS

New double-layered, two-coloured zukin headwrap

Deepstone Scythe

Barrel cannon on each side of bike to blast ghosts

NINJA FILE

LIKES: Black armor
DISLIKES: Haunted temples
FRIENDS: Jay
FOES: Soul Archer
SKILLS: Conquering his fears to defeat ghosts
GEAR: Deepstone Scythe

SET NAME: Blaster Bike, Master Wu Dragon, Final Flight of Destiny's Bounty, Temple of Airjitzu
SET NUMBER: 70733, 70734, 70738, 70751
YEAR: 2015

DEEPSTONE BLASTER BIKE

Cole's futuristic motorcycle was built by Cyrus Borg for Cole to use to fight the Ghost Warriors.

A TRUE NINJA, Cole is calm and focused, using his combat skills and great strength to protect the ninja team against the terrifying Ghost Warriors. Overcoming his own fears, Cole always puts his friends' safety before his own.

MORRO
GHOST ELEMENTAL MASTER OF WIND

DID YOU KNOW?
Morro was banished to the Cursed Realm after his death long ago, but escaped as a ghost when Garmadon opened the portal to unleash the Anacondrai Generals.

Bandana to hide identity

Ninja gi bearing the Golden Power emblem

Transparent green ghost legs

NINJA FILE
....

LIKES: Proving Wu wrong
DISLIKES: Taking selfies, losing the Realm Crystal
FRIENDS: Soul Archer
FOES: Lloyd
SKILLS: Airjitzu
GEAR: Howling Whip

SET NAME: Final Flight of Destiny's Bounty, Airjitzu Morro Flyer
SET NUMBER: 70738, 70743
YEAR: 2015

Ragged black cape

PERFECT STUDENT
Morro was Master Wu's first student. He soon mastered the martial arts and Wu thought that he might be the prophesied Green Ninja. When it became clear that he wasn't, Morro became obsessed with proving Wu wrong.

BACK FROM THE CURSED REALM as a ghost, Morro is set on revenge against Wu and the ninja. Driven by jealousy, Morro uses his cunning and mastery of his element, the wind, to possess Lloyd and attack the ninja. His mission is to bring evil to Ninjago Island once again.

MORRO'S DRAGON

POSSESSED ELEMENTAL WIND DRAGON

Large articulated fabric wings

DID YOU KNOW?

Unlike the other ghost dragons, who only have ethereal snake-like bodies, Morro's possessed dragon has limbs and vicious claws, too.

Saddle has giant claw decorations with neon steering ghost chain.

Huge brick-built, posable head with opening fang-filled jaw

ARTICULATED MONSTER

Morro's dragon is a frightening sight with its neon fangs and claws. The beast's legs, feet, and whip-like tail have full articulation with ball hinges.

MORRO'S ONCE BENIGN

earthly elemental Wind Dragon is now a ferocious and vile ghost beast. The mighty creature is completely under Morro's dark control and will do whatever his evil master bids him to do, capturing his victims in his huge fang-filled jaws.

MASTER WU

IN RETIREMENT

NINJA FILE

LIKES: Happy customers
DISLIKES: Power-hungry pupils who turn evil
FRIENDS: Misako
FOES: Morro
SKILLS: Brewing tea, banishing ghosts
GEAR: Deepstone Staff

SET NAME: Master Wu Dragon
SET NUMBER: 70734
YEAR: 2015

Separate long beard and mustache

Flaming teapot

Deepstone Staff

DID YOU KNOW?

Master Wu's tea shop is called Steep Wisdom. It is located in a valley on Ninjago Island and has a tea farm and pond behind it.

TEA SHOP BREAK-IN

When the Ghost Warriors attack Wu's tea farm and shop, he comes out of retirement to help his ninja battle the attackers.

AFTER MASTER WU RETIRES, he opens a tea shop with the help of Nya and Misako. The wise old ninja enjoys drinking tea and sharing stories with his customers. However, his teaching days aren't entirely over— between cups of tea he trains Nya to become the Water Ninja.

MASTER WU's DRAGON

ELEMENTAL CREATION DRAGON

Golden body armor made from conical hats

Detachable box saddle

Dragon features a large mustache and bushy eyebrows like its master.

NINJA FILE

LIKES: Being summoned
DISLIKES: Ghost poison
FRIENDS: Master Wu
FOES: Soul Archer
SKILLS: Firing missiles
GEAR: Fearsome jaws

SET NAME: Master Wu Dragon
SET NUMBER: 70734
YEAR: 2015

THIS MYSTICAL CREATURE

is Master Wu's first Elemental Dragon. Even though he has had the skills to summon it for years, Wu calls on it for the first time to inspire Nya to become the Master of Water. He later calls on the beast to aid in the ninja's battles with the Ghost Warriors.

WOOF, WOOF!

Master Wu gets himself a pet dog when he retires. The dog helps him guard the tea shop and farm and Wu has even made him a special wheeled carriage to carry a crossbow!

RONIN
MERCENARY AND THIEF

One of two Deepstone swords with shoulder scabbard

Cybernetic eyepiece and cloth patch

NINJA FILE

LIKES: Stealing
DISLIKES: Losing bets
FRIENDS: Who needs friends when you can make money?
FOES: Everyone
SKILLS: Stealing, altering memories, piloting airships
GEAR: Stud shooters

SET NAME:
Ronin R.E.X.
SET NUMBER: 70735
YEAR: 2015

RONIN'S R.E.X.
Ronin is master of the skies in his awesome two-in-one airship. Equipped with an arsenal of weapons and a detachable Airjitzu flyer, Ronin is more than a match for the Ghost Warriors.

MOTIVATED BY GREED and money, the self-centred Ronin will do anyone's dirty work as long as he gets paid. Dressed in stolen samurai armor and wielding two guns and two swords, Ronin is smart and ruthless. This thief knows how to get his own way in any situation.

NINJA NYA
ELEMENTAL MASTER OF WATER

Two-layered zukin ninja headwrap

Sashes with new elemental water emblem

DID YOU KNOW?
Nya inherited the elemental power of water from her mother.

NYA'S AIRBIKE
This ninja has what it takes! Astride her sleek airbike, black hair blowing free in the wind, the Water Ninja can fend off the attacking ghouls, skillfully wielding her Deepstone katana and sai.

INTUITIVE NYA is back and is fulfilling her destiny! Under Master Wu's tutorship, Nya finds her inner ninja and learns to control her elemental power, water. Using hydrokinesis, this super warrior can manipulate and generate water, for a splash of serious girl power!

BANSHA
BLADE MASTER

NINJA FILE

LIKES: Screaming
DISLIKES: Earplugs
FRIENDS: Ghost Warriors
FOES: Traitor Ronin
SKILLS: Telepathy, possession, killer scream
GEAR: Dual Ghost Master Blades

SET NAME: Jay Walker One, Titan Mech Battle, Final Flight of Destiny's Bounty
SET NUMBER: 70731, 70737, 70738
YEAR: 2015

Translucent neon female ghost headpiece

DID YOU KNOW?
Bansha's name and powers are a reference to the mythical Banshee, the wailing female spirit of folklore.

Beneath his armor, Bansha has red sleeves.

Tattered robe with leather strap holding a jagged-blade knife at the front and two shurikens at the back

Trans-neon ghostly trail instead of leg piece

GHOSTLY X MECH!
The Ghost Warriors possess Nya's Samurai X Mech and turn it into their own ghostly battle machine: Mech-enstein! With Bansha at the helm, they attack the ninja.

Hinged, posable legs and feet support the rotating Mech torso

WITH A WAILING, high-pitched scream that can shatter eardrums and cause avalanches, the Ghost Warrior Bansha is a terrifying and dangerous ethereal force. She can take over someone's body and mind from a distant location.

GHOULTAR

SCYTHE MASTER

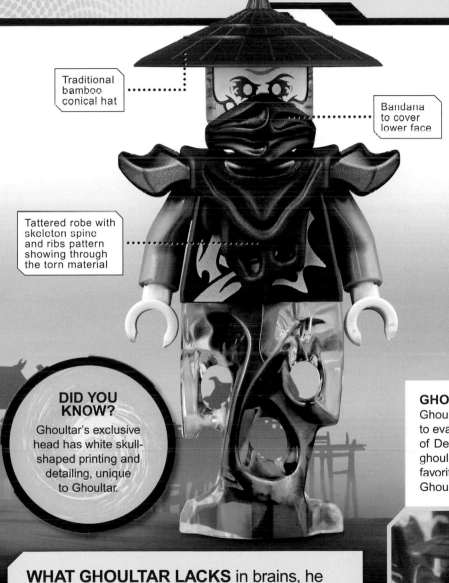

Traditional bamboo conical hat

Bandana to cover lower face

Tattered robe with skeleton spine and ribs pattern showing through the torn material

NINJA FILE

LIKES: Dancing
DISLIKES: Getting trapped
FRIENDS: Bansha
FOES: Nya and Ronin
SKILLS: Strength—ghosts go to the gym too!
GEAR: Scythe Ghost Master Blade

SET NAME: City of Stiix, Ronin R.E.X., Titan Mech Battle, Final Flight of Destiny's Bounty
SET NUMBER: 70732, 70735, 70737, 70738
YEAR: 2015

DID YOU KNOW?

Ghoultar's exclusive head has white skull-shaped printing and detailing, unique to Ghoultar.

GHOSTBUSTERS!

Ghoultar's brute strength isn't enough to evade capture. Using a cage made of Deepstone, the ninja imprison the ghoul. And with the promise of his favorite Puffy Pot Stickers snack, Ghoultar is almost ready to talk!

WHAT GHOULTAR LACKS in brains, he makes up for in brute strength and his skills with the scythe. He's quick to follow orders and is a powerful warrior. Unfortunately Ghoultar has a destructive nature, and if he doesn't understand his orders he can bring disaster down on his own side!

::IRJITZU K::I

SPINNING FIRE FLYER

NINJA FILE

LIKES: Funky airjitzu moves
DISLIKES: Being beaten by a ghost master
FRIENDS: Airjitzu ninja
FOES: Ronin
SKILLS: Flying
GEAR: Blade of Wildfire

SET NAME: Airjitzu Kai Flyer
SET NUMBER: 70739
YEAR: 2015

New ninja robe with flame pattern and Kai's elemental symbol on the front and his fire emblem on the back of the torso.

SPINJITZU TO AIRJITZU

Airjitzu is an extension of the martial arts technique of Spinjitzu. By tapping deeper into his elemental energy Kai is able to create an airborne vortex of fire.

Blade of Wildfire—this triple-action weapon encompasses two scythe blades (one spiked, the other jagged) and a burning fire sword.

BY LEARNING THE ANCIENT ART of Airjitzu, Kai has reached a higher level of his true ninja potential. His new flame-patterned robe reflects this elevated status. Focusing on the power of his fire energy, Kai creates a tornado-like vortex around himself and levitates over the land. Maybe now the ninja will be a match for the ghosts.

AIRJITZU JAY

SPINNING LIGHTNING FLYER

NINJA FILE

LIKES: Cyclondo
DISLIKES: Temple traps where they're learning Airjitzu
FRIENDS: Misako, ninja
FOES: Ghastly Morro
SKILLS: Using technology
GEAR: Thunder Head

SET NAME: Airjitzu Jay Flyer
SET NUMBER: 70740
YEAR: 2015

Unique blue headpiece with lightning patterns around the eyes

Electro torch

DID YOU KNOW?

Jay decides to call the martial arts technique of Airjitzu "Cyclondo" because he thinks it sounds cooler!

MASTER OF AIRJITZU

Ghost Master Yang was the creator of the martial art form Airjitzu. He left a scroll on which he wrote down the techniques of this ancient art.

AT FIRST, the Master of Lightning struggles to focus his mind on creating enough energy to make his Airjitzu tornado. However, when Master Wu offers him wise and encouraging words, Jay finally finds his groove. The sparks fly and Jay spins up into the air at lightning speed!

::IRJITZU COL::

SPINNING EARTH FLYER

THE HAUNTED TEMPLE

Cole makes the ultimate sacrifice for his friends. It is when he goes back into the Temple of Airjitzu to retrieve the scroll revealing the secret techniques of this powerful ancient art that he is turned into a ghost.

Ninja robe with broken rock pattern

Broken rock pattern continues onto legs

Double-headed Cleaver with two scythe-like blades

COLE IS NOT HAPPY about recent events— he has been turned into a ghost! Before he can achieve the correct state of mind needed for Airjitzu, he must reconquer his fears and come to terms with his new ghost form. With a lot of reassurance from his friends, Cole is able to channel his earth element.

AIRJITZU ZANE

SPINNING ICE FLYER

NINJA FILE

LIKES: Cryokinesis
DISLIKES: Speaking in strange dialects
FRIENDS: Jay
FOES: Flies! They're a technology hazard.
SKILLS: Storing data
GEAR: Polearm

SET NAME: Airjitzu Zane Flyer
SET NUMBER: 70742
YEAR: 2015

Polearm Ice Sword with added jagged scythe blade

Ninja robe with ice shard pattern

ICE VORTEX

Airjitzu grants the user the ability to fly in a small elemental vortex for a limited time. Zane propels himself upwards using the power and energy of his element, ice.

ONE ADVANTAGE OF being a Nindroid is having a superior machine mind. Zane applies his computer logic to learning the art of Airjitzu. Before long, the cool ninja is combining his powers and channelling his freezing energies to rocket into the sky in an awesome icy tornado.

TEMPLE WU

TEA EXPERT

NINJA FILE

LIKES: Serving tea
DISLIKES: Coffee
FRIENDS: Misako
FOES: The Preeminent
SKILLS: Giving advice
GEAR: Teapot. It only appears harmless.

SET NAME: Temple of Airjitzu
SET NUMBER: 70751
YEAR: 2015

DID YOU KNOW?

The ninja have shares in Wu's tea shop. Kai gives this money to Ronin in order to save his life.

Long, gold sleeveless vest over robe with golden flower symbol on back of torso

Elaborate design continues on to legs

"T" FOR TRANQUILI-TEA

Wu couldn't think of a more idyllic way to spend his retirement than making and drinking his favorite hot beverage! While the tea brews, the old Spinjitzu Master offers his customers words of wisdom.

AFTER MANY YEARS of mentoring and teaching, the ever-patient Wu is happy to hang up his fighting robes. His stylish long vest and gi are perfect for relaxing in the new tea shop he runs with Misako. Retirement seems to be suiting Wu well, but will he be allowed to enjoy a simpler life for long?

MISAKO

ARCHEOLOGIST

Gray hair piece comes with a long French braided ponytail

Dual-sided head: one face with glasses, smile, and laughter lines; one with an amused expression

Safari-style suit with pockets, green neck bandana, and leather belt

NINJA FILE

LIKES: Painting
DISLIKES: Interruptions—an artist needs her space
FRIENDS: Wu
FOES: Ghosts and ghouls
SKILLS: Guiding ninja against ghosts
GEAR: Paintbrush

SET NAME: Temple of Airjitzu
SET NUMBER: 70751
YEAR: 2015

HIDDEN TALENT

Misako is a keen painter. When she's not researching history, helping Wu teach the ninja, or working in the tea shop, Misako relaxes by taking up her brush and putting paint to canvas. The Temple of Airjitzu set comes complete with an artist's studio.

ARTISTIC MISAKO works at the Ninjago Museum of History as an archaeologist and researcher. When the ninja go to Ninjago City to face the Stone Army, they meet Misako and discover that she is actually Lloyd's mother and Garmadon's long-lost wife.

NINJAGO MAILMAN

EXPRESS DELIVERY

DID YOU KNOW?

The mailman is a recurring background character in the NINJAGO™ TV series, but appears for the first time as a minifigure in the Temple of Airjitzu set.

Purple jacket features mail horn logo.

Letter tile with an elaborate signature

WELCOME BREAK

In the Temple of Airjitzu, the mailman is one of the many guests who enjoy watching a shadow puppet show. He sits alongside the ninja, Claire, and Jesper.

TRULY DEDICATED TO HIS JOB, the mailman goes beyond the call of duty to deliver mail to the ninja. No mountain is too high, no terrain too dangerous or bizarre, and no hideout too secret for this tireless postal hero. By air or by sea, no delivery is too distant. He is definitely a first-class chap!

DARETH
MASTER OF CHARM

NINJA FILE

LIKES: Bragging
DISLIKES: Messing up his hair
FRIENDS: Jesper
FOES: Ghosts
SKILLS: Charming others
GEAR: Shovel

SET NAME: Temple of Airjitzu
SET NUMBER: 70751
YEAR: 2015

Coiffed, glossy hair is Dareth's crowning glory!

DID YOU KNOW?

Before he became an instructor, Dareth toured Ninjago Island as a singer with a show named "Brown Suede Shoes."

Standard LEGO shovel can be used as a weapon.

New ninja robes with star pendant and star emblem on back of torso, and elaborate gold trim

LOYAL FRIEND

Dareth is always ready to go the extra mile for his ninja friends. He might not be able to protect them in a battle, but he can cook them a feast from food found in the Temple of Airjitzu and entertain them with his embellished stories!

IN SPITE OF his constant bragging and belief that he is a "legend," Dareth is a likeable guy and a loyal friend to the ninja. What he lacks in real ninja skills, he makes up for with his creative flair and his smooth charm. However, his new robes reveal he hasn't given up his obsession with medals!

JESPER

TEMPLE GROUNDSMAN

Catch of the day!

Outback-style cowboy hat worn with neck bandana

Casual safari-style shirt with smiley face badge on pocket

NINJA FILE

LIKES: A tidy temple
DISLIKES: Dirty ponds
FRIENDS: Funny Dareth
FOES: Ghosts
SKILLS: Fishing
GEAR: Fishing rod, and sometimes a fish

SET NAME: Temple of Airjitzu
SET NUMBER: 70751
YEAR: 2015

Protective apron covered in stains

FISHERMAN'S FRIEND

Jesper is a good friend of Dareth's. The competitive fishing pals can never agree on who has caught the biggest fish!

BEARDED JESPER spends his days keeping the Temple of Airjitzu shiny and clean. In his spare time he enjoys searching for the best fishing spots on Ninjago Island and trying to catch the biggest fish ever. His minifigure is kitted out accordingly, and well suited for the great outdoors.

CLAIRE
JESPER'S DAUGHTER

Claire always carries her brush with her—it makes a handy weapon!

This amulet-style necklace might bring good luck and ward off ghosts!

NINJA FILE

LIKES: Shadow-puppet shows at the temple
DISLIKES: Tangly hair
FRIENDS: Ninja, Jesper
FOES: Skreemers
SKILLS: Being friendly
GEAR: Hairbrush, glider vehicle

SET NAME: Temple of Airjitzu
SET NUMBER: 70751
YEAR: 2015

DID YOU KNOW?
Claire does not actually appear in the NINJAGO™ TV series, although her minifigure is included in the Temple of Airjitzu set.

BATWING GLIDER
Thrill-seeker Claire can hardly contain her excitement when she gets to take the Batwing Glider for a spin around the temple, especially as she gets to meet the adventurous ninja.

JESPER'S DAUGHTER, CLAIRE, has always thought that her dad's job—looking after the Temple of Airjitzu grounds—was pretty boring. But she gets a fright when she becomes embroiled in the ninja's latest adventure. Skreemers and weapon-wielding ghosts are the stuff of nightmares!

DK Penguin
Random
House

Project Editor Emma Grange
Senior Designers Jo Connor, Mark Penfound
Editors Arushi Vats, Rosie Peet, Matt Jones,
Clare Millar
Designers Radhika Banerjee, Dimple Vohra,
Stefan Georgiou
Editorial Assistants Beth Davies
Pre-Production Producer Kavita Varma
Senior Producer Lloyd Robertson
Editorial Managers Paula Regan,
Chitra Subramanyam
Design Managers Guy Harvey, Neha Ahuja
Creative Manager Sarah Harland
Art Director Lisa Lanzarini
Publisher Julie Ferris
Publishing Director Simon Beecroft

First American Edition, 2016
Published in the United States by DK Publishing
345 Hudson Street, New York, New York 10014
DK, a Division of Penguin Random House LLC

Contains content previously published in LEGO®
NINJAGO™ *Character Encyclopedia Updated and Expanded
Edition* (2016)

001–298874–Jul/16

ACKNOWLEDGEMENTS
DK would like to thank Randi Sørensen, Martin Leighton Lindhart,
Paul Hansford, Madeline Boushie, Simon Lucas, Nicolaas Johan Bernardo
Vás, and Daniel McKenna at the LEGO Group, Gary Ombler for extra
photography, Andy Jones for extra editorial help, Sam Bartlett for
design assistance and Claire Sipi for her writing. For the original edition
of this book, DK would like to thank Shari Last, Julia March, Ruth Amos,
Lauren Rosier, Mark Richards, Jon Hall, Clive Savage,
Ron Stobbart, and Catherine Saunders.

www.LEGO.com

www.dk.com
A WORLD OF IDEAS:
SEE ALL THERE IS TO KNOW